I

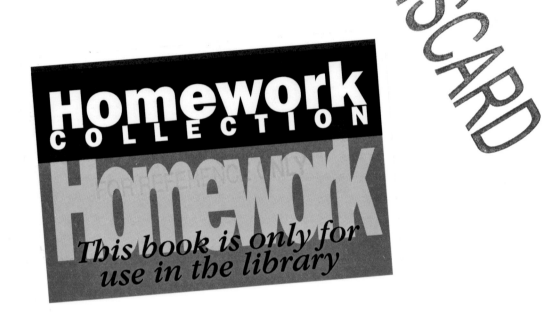

INSTRUMENTS *in* **MUSIC**

JAZZ AND BLUES

Roger Thomas

Heinemann
LIBRARY

First published in Great Britain by Heinemann Library
Halley Court, Jordan Hill, Oxford OX2 8EJ
a division of Reed Educational and Professional Publishing Ltd.
Heinemann is a registered trademark of Reed Educational and Professional Publishing Ltd.

OXFORD FLORENCE PRAGUE MADRID ATHENS
MELBOURNE AUCKLAND KUALA LUMPUR SINGAPORE TOKYO
IBADAN NAIROBI KAMPALA JOHANNESBURG GABORONE
PORTSMOUTH NH (USA) CHICAGO MEXICO CITY SAO PAULO

© Reed Educational and Professional Publishing Ltd 1998

Designed by Susan Clarke
Printed in Hong Kong

02 01 00 99 98
10 9 8 7 6 5 4 3 2 1

ISBN 0 431 08805 5

British Library Cataloguing in Publication Data

Thomas, Roger
   Jazz and blues. – (Instruments in music)
   1.Jazz – Juvenile literature 2.Blues (Music) – Juvenile literature
   3.Musical Instruments – Juvenile literature
   I.Title
   781.4'165

Acknowledgements
The Publishers would like to thank the following for permission to reproduce photographs:
Trevor Clifford, pp.10 centre, 22, 24 (Hertfordshire County Music Service), p.29 top left (Hill & Company), p.29 (Mo Clifton, Clifton Basses), pp.6, 8, 10 top and bottom, 29 top centre, top right, bottom left and bottom right (John Myatt Brass and Woodwind); Dat's Jazz Picture Library, pp.14, 17, 20, 23, 25; Liz Eddison, p.12 right and middle, pp.12 left, 28 (Hobgoblin Music); Robert Ellis, p.18; Pictorial Press, p.21; Redferns, pp.13 bottom, 19, p.4 (Max Jones Files), pp.5, 13 top (Leon Morris), pp.16, 26, 27 (David Redfern); Sylvia Pitcher Photo Library, p.15; Zefa, p.7.

Cover photograph: Tony Stone/David Ball

Our thanks to Betty Root for her comments in the preparation of this book.

Every effort has been made to contact copyright holders of any material reproduced in this book. Any omissions will be rectified in subsequent printings if notice is given to the Publisher.

CONTENTS

Some words are shown in bold, **like this**.
You can find out what they mean by looking
in the Glossary.

INTRODUCTION

Jazz and blues music was started over a hundred years ago in the USA by African-American people. They were brought from Africa to the USA as slaves. Blues songs were often about hardship or love. Jazz music had a lively sound and strong **rhythms**. It was often played by **marching bands** or at small concerts. Musicians often made up part of the music as they played. This is called improvisation.

A jazz band playing an early style of jazz

A contemporary jazz orchestra

A lot of jazz music is still played at small concerts.
However, the music is now very popular throughout the
world, so that much larger concerts also take place in big
concert halls and at jazz festivals. The instruments will
often be amplified and the audience can be very large.

THE SAXOPHONE

The saxophone was invented by a man called Adolphe Saxe in 1846. It is called a **woodwind** instrument but is usually made of metal! It makes a sound when the player blows across the **reed** in the **mouthpiece**. The player changes the **notes** with **keys** which cover holes in the instrument. The bigger saxophones play low notes and the smaller ones higher notes.

soprano

alto

tenor

baritone

There are soprano, alto, tenor and baritone saxophones

This saxophonist is playing a tenor saxophone

A person who plays a saxophone is called a saxophonist. The saxophone was first played in **marching bands**. It is now a very important instrument in jazz and blues music. It is often used as a **lead instrument** in jazz.

THE CLARINET

A person who plays the clarinet is called a clarinettist. The clarinet makes a sound when the player blows into a **mouthpiece** which has a **reed** in it. The player changes the **notes** with **keys** which cover holes in the instrument. There are several different sizes of clarinet. The bass clarinet plays lower notes. The clarinet and the bass clarinet are the two sizes most often used in jazz.

clarinet

bass clarinet

A clarinet and a bass clarinet

This musician is a clarinettist

The clarinet is a **woodwind** instrument, although clarinets can sometimes be made of plastic. The clarinet was first used in **marching band** and **classical music** over two hundred years ago. It has a soft but clear tone. It is often used as a **lead instrument** in **traditional jazz**.

BRASS INSTRUMENTS

Brass instruments are made of curly metal tubes. They make a sound when the player blows into a **mouthpiece**. The **notes** of trumpets, cornets and flugelhorns are changed by pressing **valves** on the instrument. The valves change which tubes the player's breath goes into. Trombones usually have a slide instead of valves. This is an extra tube which the player moves in and out to change the notes.

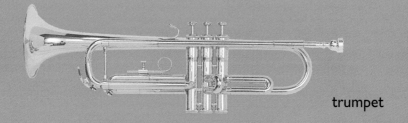

trumpet

The pictures show
a trumpet, a flugelhorn
and a trombone

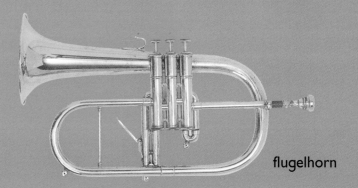

flugelhorn

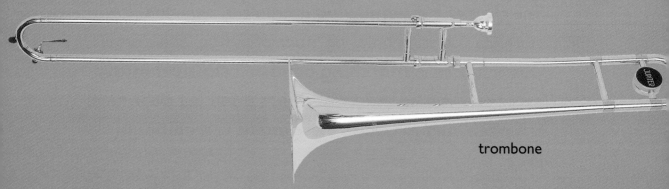

trombone

These musicians are playing a trombone and a trumpet

These brass instruments were first used in **marching bands** and orchestras. Trumpets have a bright sound and play high notes. This makes them good **lead instruments** in a jazz group. The trombone has a smoother sound and plays lower notes.

THE BANJO AND GUITAR

The banjo was developed in the USA over two hundred years ago from African string instruments. In **traditional jazz** bands the banjo is used to play **chords** which help keep the beat of the music. The banjo has a front like a drum. This makes the strings sound very loud. In modern jazz this part of the music is played on a guitar with metal strings.

banjo

archtop guitar

acoustic guitar with bottleneck

The banjo and guitar are often used in jazz. Blues guitarists often use a bottleneck to give the notes a sliding sound

Blues guitarists use guitars with steel strings too. They often play on their own and usually sing as well. Jazz guitarists can play chords, or **solos** using single notes. They do not usually sing while they play.

A traditional
jazz banjo player
and a modern
jazz guitarist

BASS INSTRUMENTS

The double bass is used to play low **notes** in jazz music. The part is often very **rhythmic** and in time with the drums. The double bass has four thick strings. The player usually plucks them with the fingers of one hand. The notes are changed by holding down the strings on different parts of the **neck**. A person who plays one of these instruments is called a bassist.

This bassist is playing a double bass. It is the same as the double bass used in an orchestra

This bassist is playing an electric bass guitar

Some jazz bassists use an electric bass guitar. It is easier to carry than a double bass. It also plays low notes but has a brighter sound. Some players use one with no **frets**, which sounds more like a double bass. In **traditional jazz**, the bass part is sometimes played on a tuba or sousaphone. These are big **brass** instruments.

THE PIANO

The piano is a very important instrument in jazz and blues. It is either played **solo** or as part of a group. It is played in many different **styles** of jazz. A person who plays a piano is called a pianist.

This pianist is playing in a jazz piano trio

Blues pianists will often play on their own. Sometimes they sing as well

Blues piano music can often sound sad. This is because blues tunes and songs are usually about hardship or problems which have happened in the musician's life.

OTHER KEYBOARD INSTRUMENTS

Modern jazz players sometimes use **electric** or **electronic** keyboards, such as the electric piano. The electric piano is easy to carry to concerts. It must be played through an **amplifier**. It has a softer sound than an ordinary piano.

Playing the electric piano

The electric organ is also a popular jazz and blues keyboard instrument

The electric organ has a big warm sound. Many players prefer to use old electric organs for this reason, even though there are now many other kinds of electric or electronic keyboard instruments.

THE DRUM KIT

The jazz drummer usually keeps the **rhythm** and speed of the music steady. However, in modern jazz, he or she will often add lots of changes to the rhythm. The drums are played with sticks or with brushes made from wire or plastic. Some jazz drummers also use other percussion instruments, such as cowbells and woodblocks, to add different kinds of sounds to their playing.

This drummer is playing a modern jazz drum kit

When jazz music first started, drum kits looked like this

When musicians first started to play jazz, drum kits were often made up from drums and percussion instruments used in other kinds of music or from other countries. These could include **bass drums** and **snare drums** used by **marching bands** or **classical** orchestras, other drums from Africa or China and Turkish and Chinese **cymbals**.

PERCUSSION

A large jazz group will sometimes have a percussionist as well as a drummer. The percussionist adds lots of extra **rhythms** and types of sound to the music. The sounds can include extra drum beats, woodblock sounds and shaking and rattling sounds from tambourines and maracas.

All these percussion instruments can be used in jazz

timbales

congas

temple blocks

guiro

bongos

claves

This Latin jazz percussionist is playing timbales and other percussion instruments

There are different kinds of jazz from all over the world. Percussion is very important in **Latin jazz** and **Afro-jazz**. In some new jazz music, objects such as dustbins, chains and springs can be used as percussion.

THE VIBRAPHONE

Tuned percussion instruments have metal or wooden bars which are laid out like the **keys** on a piano. Unlike other percussion instruments, they can play lots of different **notes**. They are usually played with soft **mallets**. The player will often hold two mallets in each hand. The most popular tuned percussion instrument used in jazz is the vibraphone. It is usually played as a **lead instrument** in a small jazz group.

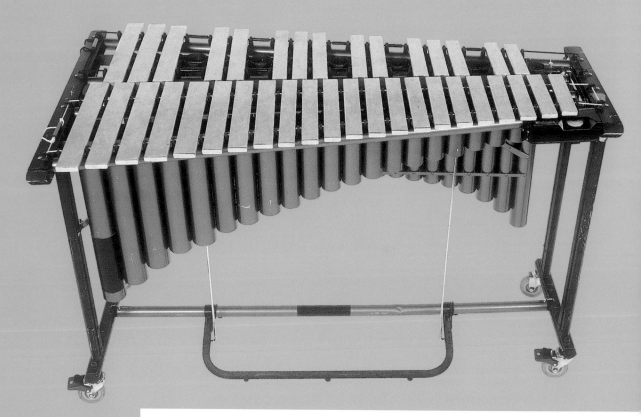

The vibraphone is a tuned percussion instrument sometimes heard in jazz music

This musician is playing a vibraphone

The bars on a vibraphone have tubes underneath them. Each tube has a small fan at the bottom. The fans are turned slowly by an electric motor. This gives the instrument a soft, echoing sound.

JAZZ AND BLUES SINGING

Jazz singing can be very exciting. It is usually performed by a **solo** singer with a band. Jazz singing can be happy, sad, exciting or gentle. Sometimes jazz singers will sing made-up sounds instead of words. This is called scatting.

A jazz singer

This blues musician is singing while playing the guitar

Some blues singers sing with a band but many blues singers just use a guitar or piano. Sometimes a singing blues guitarist will also play an harmonica to add instrumental solos to a song.

THE HARMONICA AND OTHER INSTRUMENTS

The harmonica was developed from a Chinese instrument called the sheng. The harmonica has metal **reeds** inside it which make a sound when the player blows into the instrument. It became popular in blues music as it is cheap, easy to carry and can be played with a sad tone which suits the music's **style**.

The harmonica is widely used in blues music. A blues harmonica is often called a harp, although it has nothing in common with the string instrument of that name

violin

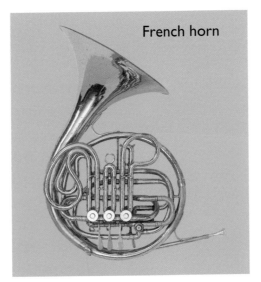

French horn

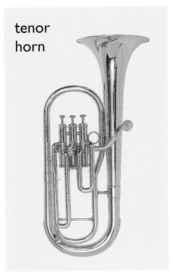

tenor horn

oboe

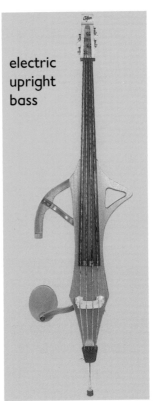

electric upright bass

tuba

People who write or play jazz often like to bring new ideas into the music. One way of doing this is by playing or writing music for different instruments. The instruments on this page are unusual as jazz instruments but they have all been included in jazz bands.

GLOSSARY

Afro-jazz a type of jazz which uses ideas directly from African music

amplifier an electrical device which makes sound louder

bass drum a drum with a low sound

brass a hard metal used to make some wind instruments

chords several notes played at once

classical music traditional concert music started in Europe and often played by orchestras

cymbals two brass discs which are hit together or with a stick

electric a type of instrument with a quiet sound which is made louder by an amplifier

electronic a type of instrument which makes sounds using electrical current.

frets strips of wire on the neck of guitars and banjos which the player holds the string against when choosing notes

keys metal buttons on woodwind instruments which the player presses to change the notes

Latin jazz a type of jazz started in South America

lead instrument the instrument in a group which plays the main tune

marching bands military bands which usually play very rhythmic music

mallets soft-headed sticks

mouthpiece the part of a wind instrument which the player blows into

neck the long part of a stringed instrument with the strings stretched along it

notes musical sounds

reed a thin piece of cane or metal in a mouthpiece which makes a sound when air is blown across it

rhythms patterns of notes in music

snare drums drums with wires underneath them which make a buzzing sound when the drums are hit

solo one musician playing

styles particular ways of playing music

traditional jazz a type of jazz which is like the earliest kind played

valves buttons on a brass instrument which help to change the notes

woodwind wind instruments other than brass

FURTHER READING

Live Music! Elizabeth Sharma. Wayland, 1992

You may need help to read these other titles on music.

Eyewitness Kit: Music. Dorling Kindersley, 1993

How the World Makes Music. Iwo Zaluski and Pamela Zaluski. Young Library, 1994

The World of Music: With CD. Nicola Barber and Mary Mure. Evans Brothers, 1994

INDEX